While every precaution has been taken in the preparation of this book, the publisher assumes no responsibility for errors or omissions, or for damages resulting from the use of the information contained herein.

FROM SILENCE TO ACTION: WHITE MEN'S JOURNEY IN SOCIAL JUSTICE

First edition. November 9, 2024.

Copyright © 2024 Timothy Rodgers.

ISBN: 979-8227133601

Written by Timothy Rodgers.

Table of Contents

From Silence to Action: White Men's Journey in Social Justice 1

Introduction 3

Chapter 1: Historical Context: Power, Privilege, and the Legacy of Inequality 7

Chapter 2: Reexamining Identity: Who Am I in This? 13

Chapter 3: Listening as an Act of Engagement 19

Chapter 4: The Intersection of Race and Gender: Breaking Down Barriers 25

Chapter 5: Redefining Masculinity and Privilege 31

Chapter 6: Case Studies of Allyship and Resistance 37

Chapter 7: Facing Backlash and Controversy 43

Chapter 8: A Vision for the Future 49

Chapter 9: The Journey Toward Social Justice 55

"The moment we believe we have all the answers is the moment we stop growing and adapting. When we assume certainty, we close ourselves off to new ideas, perspectives, and solutions. In that moment, we become stagnant, unable to respond to the evolving needs of the world around us. True effectiveness comes from humility—acknowledging that there is always more to learn, more to understand, and more work to be done. It is in our willingness to question, adapt, and collaborate that we remain dynamic and impactful. Only through constant reflection and openness can we continue to make a meaningful difference."

Timothy Rodgers

From Silence to Action: White Men's Journey in Social Justice

By Timothy Rodgers

Introduction

In the modern era, the conversations around social justice, racial equality, gender rights, and personal identity have evolved into movements that are reshaping society at its core. These movements reach into our institutions, our media, and even our daily interactions, challenging us to re-evaluate long-standing assumptions and beliefs. They demand that we confront the impact of history and the weight of deeply ingrained social systems. The streets of Selma, Stonewall, Ferguson, and many other places have become historic symbols of struggle, and today's protests, marches, social media campaigns, and educational initiatives echo those legacies while breaking new ground. We are living in an era of reckoning, where individuals and groups are being called to address inequalities and injustices, asking not only how they experience these realities but also what role they play in changing them.

For white men, these shifts raise a complex and sometimes uncomfortable question: *What role do white men play in these movements, both historically and today?* In a world that increasingly demands accountability, awareness, and allyship, white men are being asked to examine the privileges they may carry and the influence they wield within these social spaces. This question doesn't have a simple answer. It's a question that touches on historical privilege, modern systems of power, personal identity, and collective responsibility. The aim of this book is not to vilify, exonerate, or simplify white men's roles in these movements but to explore them in all their complexity, examining how they have contributed to both the challenges and the progress within these movements.

Rather than proposing a single perspective, this book takes a nuanced view, looking at both the positive contributions and systemic challenges that white men face when engaging in social justice. History reveals many examples of white men who have used their positions of power to advocate for equality and justice, standing alongside marginalized groups in their fight for rights. Abolitionists like John Brown, civil rights allies like Andrew Goodman, and feminists like John Stuart Mill have all demonstrated how white men can be powerful agents for change. Yet the historical record also shows the ways in which white male privilege has reinforced inequality and perpetuated oppression, whether consciously or unconsciously. The truth is that privilege can distort perspectives, and it often shields individuals from recognizing the hardships that marginalized groups face. This book seeks to illuminate both sides of that coin, understanding how white men's positions of privilege can both help and hinder movements for equality.

Part of this complexity lies in the concept of allyship. What does it mean for a white man to be an ally in movements that demand racial justice, gender equity, and the dismantling of systemic privilege? Allyship is more than just holding progressive beliefs; it requires active listening, self-reflection, and a willingness to engage in sometimes uncomfortable conversations. True allyship often involves stepping back, creating space for voices that have long been silenced, and being willing to support movements without centering oneself within them. This book examines allyship as an evolving practice, not a fixed identity, recognizing that it is a journey requiring continual self-awareness and commitment.

White men who seek to engage with these movements often face a number of internal and external challenges. Internally, they may grapple with feelings of guilt, confusion, or defensiveness, as confronting one's privilege and role in perpetuating inequality is rarely a straightforward process. Externally, they may encounter resistance from others who are skeptical of their motives or question their ability to truly understand the struggles of marginalized communities. This book acknowledges these challenges and seeks to offer guidance on how white men can navigate them in a way that is constructive and grounded in genuine commitment to change.

Furthermore, historical privilege and societal roles profoundly shape the way white men interact with these movements. For generations, societal norms placed white men in positions of authority, where they made decisions that shaped public policy, economics, and culture. This historical context means that white men who choose to support social justice movements must understand that their roles carry unique responsibilities. In many ways, they have the opportunity to influence others within their communities, but they must also be mindful of the legacy of power they inherit and avoid replicating old patterns of dominance.

Throughout this book, we will explore the diverse ways in which white men can become allies in the pursuit of a more equitable world. We will examine the obstacles they encounter, from confronting personal biases to navigating societal expectations, and we will consider how these challenges can be transformed into opportunities for growth. By understanding the role of white men within social, racial, gender, and identity movements, we can begin to build a model for allyship that is rooted in respect, humility, and accountability.

This book invites readers to step into the complex, sometimes uncomfortable, but ultimately rewarding journey of allyship, with the hope that each reader might come away with a clearer understanding of what it means to support a world where equality is not merely an ideal, but a reality.

Chapter 1: Historical Context: Power, Privilege, and the Legacy of Inequality

Understanding the role of white men in today's social movements requires a journey through history, examining the structures of power, privilege, and inequality that have shaped societies across centuries. White men have often occupied positions of dominance in economic, political, and social spheres, with institutions and cultural norms crafted to reinforce their authority. This chapter seeks to establish the historical foundation of white male privilege and explore the legacies that continue to influence present-day social justice movements.

From the colonial era to the industrial revolution, and through the expansion of Western empires, systems were designed to favor white men while marginalizing other groups—particularly people of color and women. The ripple effects of these systems have impacted societies for generations, creating deeply ingrained patterns of inequality. As we explore this history, we see that the privilege of white men is not simply a product of individual actions or beliefs but is deeply embedded in societal institutions, cultural norms, and economic systems.

The concept of racial privilege has its roots in the colonial era, a period defined by European powers expanding their territories and exploiting the resources and people of other continents. European settlers and colonizers, driven by economic incentives and a belief in their own superiority, justified their dominance through an ideology of racial hierarchy. This ideology framed white, European men as inherently superior to the Indigenous populations they encountered and the African people they enslaved and transported to the Americas.

The economic structures that emerged during this time were explicitly built upon racial privilege. In the Americas, the Atlantic slave trade became the backbone of colonial economies. The unpaid labor of enslaved Africans generated vast wealth for white landowners and European businesses, embedding a racial economic hierarchy that would persist for centuries. This racialized labor system was legitimized through pseudoscientific beliefs about racial superiority, which were used to justify and perpetuate the exploitation and subjugation of Black people.

White male privilege was also reinforced by legal systems, with laws enacted to maintain racial boundaries and the privileges of white men. For instance, in the United States, laws forbidding interracial marriage, as well as those that classified enslaved people as property rather than humans, underscored a system that placed white men in positions of control while depriving people of color of fundamental rights. The legacy of these laws continues to echo in today's racial inequalities, as structural disparities in wealth, education, and criminal justice can all be traced back to these roots.

Just as racial privilege became entrenched through colonialism, gender-based privilege was codified through patriarchal structures that restricted women's rights and reinforced male dominance. Patriarchy was not a new concept—it had existed in various forms across societies for centuries—but colonial and industrial expansion further embedded it in Western society, often to devastating effect.

White men's dominance in the public sphere was mirrored by a limitation on women's rights and freedoms. Women, particularly white women, were confined to the domestic sphere, denied the right to vote, own property, or participate in government. In many ways, the identity of white men was built on this framework of control: to be a man was to occupy a space of authority, while women were expected to serve as subordinates. Gender roles became rigid, with expectations that men would lead and women would follow, and these norms permeated all aspects of society, from family structures to workplaces.

The Industrial Revolution further exacerbated these dynamics. While it created opportunities for economic mobility and innovation, industrialization also reinforced gender inequality by relegating women to lower-paying, less-valued work, often within factories or domestic labor. Men, particularly white men, retained the higher-status roles in management and ownership, benefiting disproportionately from economic growth. This industrial patriarchy entrenched gender hierarchies that would take centuries to dismantle, and it laid the groundwork for modern gender inequality.

The social construction of whiteness and masculinity as ideals that set white men apart from—and, by implication, above—other groups was a critical aspect of Western identity formation. Whiteness was defined not only as a racial category but also as a set of cultural and moral standards that distinguished Europeans from the Indigenous people, enslaved Africans, and other "others" who were deemed inferior. Laws and social norms that defined who could be considered "white" shaped both individual and collective identity, with white men at the top of this racial hierarchy.

This idealized whiteness was closely tied to conceptions of masculinity, which prized strength, authority, and control. White men were often portrayed as the "civilizing" force in a world that, from their perspective, was otherwise chaotic and "savage." In the United States, for instance, the concept of "Manifest Destiny" positioned white men as the natural leaders who would tame and govern a vast continent. This sense of mission not only justified violent conquests and dispossession of Indigenous peoples but also reinforced the idea of white male supremacy as a moral imperative.

White male identity was further shaped by religious, legal, and cultural norms that positioned them as natural leaders, providers, and defenders of society. As industrialization progressed, this identity shifted somewhat to incorporate values of individualism, entrepreneurial spirit, and financial success, but the foundation of authority remained intact. Even as some men began to advocate for social reforms or women's rights, mainstream identity for white men was still deeply rooted in a sense of entitlement to power and leadership, which many internalized as a natural birthright.

The boundaries of white male identity were maintained by excluding those who did not fit within its definitions of race and gender. This exclusion was not merely theoretical; it was reinforced by systems that actively marginalized groups that fell outside these categories. Immigration policies in the United States, for example, restricted entry for people deemed "unassimilable," particularly from non-European countries, while policies of segregation and redlining perpetuated racial and economic divisions.

Gender was similarly policed, with white men at the center of decision-making and social organization. Men who did not conform to heteronormative standards, or who challenged traditional masculinity, faced stigma and discrimination. Similarly, any push for gender equality was often seen as a threat to the established order, which had placed white men as the primary authority figures. The historical boundaries around whiteness and masculinity thus not only shaped identity but also functioned to maintain social hierarchies.

The accumulation of wealth through exploitation is one of the most enduring legacies of white male privilege. Colonialism and slavery generated immense wealth that enriched white men and laid the foundation for Western economies, creating disparities that persist to this day. The plantation economy in the American South, the exploitation of Indigenous lands, and the industrialization that relied on cheap, often immigrant labor, all contributed to a structure where wealth flowed upward to a small elite, predominantly composed of white men.

Economic policies throughout the 19th and 20th centuries continued to favor white men, from land grants that excluded people of color to labor laws that allowed for discriminatory hiring practices. Even as civil rights movements gained ground in the mid-20th century, these economic disparities proved difficult to dismantle, as wealth and power had already accumulated within white communities.

Legal and political systems have historically reinforced the privileges of white men by excluding others from positions of influence. The right to vote, own property, and run for office was long restricted to white men, who used their positions within government to pass laws that protected their interests and maintained racial and gendered hierarchies. These laws limited the economic, social, and political agency of marginalized groups and shaped a political landscape that privileged the status quo.

Even after legal progress was made, particularly through the civil rights movements of the 20th century, institutional inequalities persisted. Access to education, health care, and housing continued to be impacted by policies that had long favored white men, creating barriers that prevented others from achieving the same level of social mobility. Redlining, school segregation, and discriminatory lending practices, for example, all contributed to the ongoing economic divide between white men and marginalized groups, ensuring that the legacy of inequality continued.

This historical overview provides a foundation for understanding the challenges and responsibilities that white men face in modern social movements. Recognizing the roots of racial and gender privilege, the formation of white male identity, and the economic and political systems that have reinforced their power, allows us to understand the unique position that white men occupy today. This historical framework will guide our exploration of how white men can engage meaningfully in social justice, moving from a legacy of privilege to a commitment to equality and justice.

Chapter 2: Reexamining Identity: Who Am I in This?

In recent years, the roles of masculinity and whiteness have come under intense examination. For many white men, this shift has raised personal, difficult questions about identity and place in a world that increasingly demands accountability and self-awareness. What does it mean to be a white man in a landscape where racial justice, gender equality, and allyship are no longer fringe issues but essential topics for any meaningful conversation about the future? How can one reconcile a sense of self with societal expectations that call for change? This chapter explores the journey many white men face as they confront these evolving definitions of self and society. It's an inward journey of self-reflection and often discomfort, challenging traditional notions of masculinity and whiteness and redefining what it means to be an ally in today's world.

For generations, society taught white men to see their identities as "neutral" or "default"—a baseline from which other identities deviated. This "neutral" view, often subconscious, was shaped by privilege. Social structures, whether in education, employment, or media, typically centered white male perspectives, allowing white men to see themselves without the burden of race and gender dynamics constantly influencing their self-perception. Unlike people of color, women, or marginalized gender identities, who had to adapt to a system that didn't necessarily include or reflect their experiences, white men rarely needed to consider how their identity shaped their access to power and resources.

However, this privilege has not always been a source of empowerment for white men on a personal level. It has also created a significant blind spot. Privilege can make it challenging for individuals to recognize the inequities others experience. For some, it may even create a sense of entitlement or defensiveness when asked to examine their role within these structures. This expectation to "look inward" can feel jarring, especially for those who have never before been called to question their identity in the context of systemic inequality.

The context of privilege also raises questions of responsibility. The modern social landscape demands that white men reconsider their place in society—not just as individuals, but as inheritors of a legacy of racial and gender privilege. This does not mean feeling shame or guilt for being a white man; rather, it involves understanding the broader historical and societal forces that have afforded certain advantages and acknowledging that these advantages influence interactions with others.

Reexamining identity in this way is often painful, as it confronts core beliefs about fairness, merit, and individuality. Many white men may feel disoriented as they confront the reality that their success, access to opportunities, or daily interactions may not have been as impartial as they believed. Yet, this awareness is also an opportunity for growth, creating a more honest and inclusive identity that seeks to understand rather than overlook the lives and challenges of others.

Masculinity and whiteness are more than personal characteristics—they are social identities shaped by cultural, historical, and structural influences. Traditional notions of masculinity often encourage strength, self-reliance, control, and dominance, traits that, while not inherently harmful, can become restrictive or damaging when left unexamined. Within white, Western culture, masculinity has long been associated with authority, economic success, and societal control. When combined with whiteness, this masculinity becomes not only powerful but "normalized" within social structures, often at the expense of other identities.

As social justice movements emphasize the importance of diversity and dismantling systemic oppression, the intersection of whiteness and masculinity has faced increasing scrutiny. While men of other racial backgrounds also contend with questions of masculinity, white men face the additional question of whiteness—a racial identity that, historically, has held the most social power in many Western societies. Unlike Black masculinity, which has been stigmatized, criminalized, or marginalized, white masculinity has traditionally been the standard against which others are measured. For many white men, this realization can be unsettling, as it requires confronting the idea that the traits society has upheld as "strong" or "successful" are partly rooted in structures that exclude or undermine others.

In this light, masculinity is not just about individual behavior but also about social expectations and hierarchies. For instance, the idea that men should be "providers" and "protectors" has shaped expectations in the family, workplace, and society at large, often sidelining other identities and contributions. White men who hold these roles may feel conflicted about how to balance these traditional ideas of masculinity with the call to become allies in gender and racial justice movements, where collaboration, vulnerability, and listening are prized over control or dominance.

The intersection of masculinity and whiteness can also make it challenging for white men to engage openly in dialogues on race and gender. Fear of being misunderstood or appearing weak can create a barrier, reinforcing the internalized idea that vulnerability is a failure rather than a strength. Yet, allyship often requires this very openness and vulnerability. For white men to become true allies, they must redefine masculinity as a strength that includes listening, learning, and supporting rather than dominating or controlling. In this sense, masculinity becomes a flexible identity, one that adapts and grows to reflect values of equality and empathy.

Allyship is often misunderstood as a static label—something one either "is" or "is not." But true allyship is far more complex. It is not a destination; it is a journey, a continual process of learning, reflection, and adjustment. For white men, seeing allyship as a process is crucial because it shifts the focus from achieving a fixed state of "wokeness" or "progressiveness" to engaging in a continuous cycle of growth.

At its core, allyship requires humility. White men who wish to support racial justice, gender equality, or identity movements must recognize that they are entering a space where they are not the experts. It means learning from the voices of those who have lived experiences of oppression and actively seeking ways to support their needs and goals rather than imposing their own views. Effective allyship involves being aware of one's limitations and understanding that mistakes will happen. What's more, it involves actively seeking to learn from those mistakes rather than allowing them to create shame or guilt that might lead to disengagement.

Seeing allyship as a process also requires a commitment to self-education. Rather than expecting others, particularly people of color or women, to explain every nuance of injustice or oppression, true allies make an effort to educate themselves on history, social systems, and the perspectives of those who are marginalized. This self-driven learning helps ensure that allyship is not a superficial label but a deeply held commitment to understanding and action.

Perhaps most importantly, recognizing allyship as a process means accepting that there will always be room for growth. As societal awareness of justice and equality evolves, so too must allyship. What worked ten years ago may not be effective today, and what feels supportive today may need to be reexamined in the future. White men who embrace this evolution will find that allyship is not a burden but a source of personal growth and fulfillment, as it encourages them to continually reimagine their roles in the world in ways that are more inclusive, understanding, and empathetic.

The journey of reexamining identity—of asking, *Who am I in this?*—is not easy, especially for white men who must confront deeply embedded structures of privilege, masculinity, and racial identity. But this journey is essential for meaningful engagement in social justice movements. By understanding how privilege shapes identity, redefining masculinity as a source of empathy rather than control, and embracing allyship as an ongoing process, white men can become more effective allies and active contributors to the world's progress toward justice and equality.

The goal of this chapter is not to create a "perfect ally" or to suggest that anyone can transcend their biases entirely. Instead, it invites white men to embrace their identities in new ways—to recognize both the privileges and responsibilities that come with them and to navigate these identities with a sense of accountability and openness. This path of self-reflection is about learning, growing, and ultimately becoming better equipped to support the voices and struggles of those around us.

Chapter 3: Listening as an Act of Engagement

Listening is an act of engagement, an active decision to open oneself to the experiences, voices, and insights of others. For anyone striving to be an ally in social, racial, gender, and identity movements, listening is not merely a passive activity but a critical skill that must be continuously refined and practiced. In social justice work, where the voices of marginalized communities need amplification and understanding, the role of a listener is fundamental. For white men in particular, who have historically occupied positions of privilege and power, this listening requires an additional layer of humility, self-reflection, and willingness to face potentially uncomfortable truths.

Listening might appear deceptively simple, yet it is one of the most powerful acts an ally can offer. For white men, especially, listening is an important starting point because it disrupts the conventional dynamics of authority. In many cases, white men have been socialized to speak up, take charge, and assume positions of leadership. This conditioning can lead to a reflexive desire to provide solutions, assert opinions, or steer conversations. However, in social movements centered around the lived experiences of marginalized groups, the role of an ally is to shift from leading to supporting, from speaking to listening.

At its core, listening allows allies to approach these movements with humility. Rather than assuming an understanding of others' experiences, a genuine ally listens to understand rather than to respond. This means setting aside one's preconceived notions, suspending judgments, and being open to perspectives that might challenge personal beliefs or worldviews. For example, a white man may feel he understands racial issues from books he has read or classes he has taken, but active listening requires a willingness to set aside even that knowledge to fully hear the lived experiences of people of color without overlaying his own interpretations.

Listening as a first step to allyship also means confronting the limits of one's own perspective. White men have often been shielded from the impact of systemic racism, sexism, and other forms of discrimination, and may not naturally recognize the breadth of these issues in daily life. Listening to those who live with these realities broadens an ally's understanding, helping them see the nuances of privilege and oppression. Listening becomes the foundation for empathy, as allies begin to grasp the depth of challenges that marginalized individuals face. For example, listening to a Black colleague's experience with racial profiling or hearing a woman's experience with workplace discrimination allows an ally to connect on a deeper level and understand the urgency of the issues beyond an intellectual understanding.

Active listening requires emotional intelligence, which involves not only understanding one's emotions but also managing them effectively in order to respond in a way that respects and honors the other person's experiences. This is especially important when confronting social and racial injustice, as such conversations often bring up uncomfortable feelings, including guilt, defensiveness, or even shame. White men may find it challenging to listen without interjecting or becoming defensive, particularly when they feel that their character or intentions are being questioned. However, emotional intelligence helps an ally to sit with discomfort, remain open, and resist the impulse to center themselves in the conversation.

Emotional intelligence in listening means acknowledging and reflecting on one's own reactions without allowing them to dominate the conversation. When a person from a marginalized community shares their experience of discrimination, an emotionally intelligent listener recognizes that their role is not to counter, defend, or explain away the injustice, but to provide a supportive, validating presence. Emotional intelligence enables white men to resist the impulse to shift the conversation to their own experiences or to find ways to avoid personal discomfort by intellectualizing or minimizing the other person's feelings.

For example, consider a conversation where a Black colleague shares a story about an instance of racial profiling. An emotionally intelligent response would avoid platitudes like "I can't believe that still happens" or "I'm sure they didn't mean it that way." Instead, it would involve recognizing the colleague's emotions, validating their experiences, and expressing empathy in a way that centers the colleague's perspective. Responses such as, "That must have been incredibly painful," or "Thank you for sharing that with me," demonstrate an understanding that the ally's role is to bear witness, not to diminish or dismiss the experience.

Moreover, emotional intelligence allows allies to respond constructively to criticism, a crucial aspect of growth in allyship. In movements for social justice, allies may sometimes receive feedback that their actions, however well-intentioned, were harmful or misguided. Emotional intelligence helps an ally accept such feedback with humility and a desire to learn rather than defensiveness. By listening without resistance and embracing critique as an opportunity for growth, white men can become stronger allies and develop a deeper understanding of the complexities of oppression and privilege.

Listening as an ally is not only about hearing others but also about creating space for their voices to be heard. This involves actively supporting and amplifying marginalized voices, recognizing that these perspectives are often silenced or overlooked in mainstream conversations. For white men, creating space may mean stepping back to allow others to speak, ensuring that marginalized voices are not only included but prioritized in conversations about social justice.

Creating space for marginalized voices can take many forms. In a professional setting, it may mean refraining from speaking up in a meeting to allow a person of color to share their perspective. On social media, it may involve sharing articles, posts, or videos created by activists from marginalized communities instead of posting one's own thoughts on an issue. In personal conversations, it could mean recognizing when one's own experiences or insights are less relevant and intentionally shifting the focus to the experiences of those who are directly affected by the issue.

Creating space also involves using one's privilege to support and elevate the voices of marginalized individuals. For example, if a white man is in a leadership position, he might advocate for hiring practices that diversify the voices and perspectives within his organization. If he's part of a community group, he might suggest inviting speakers from marginalized backgrounds to share their experiences. It also means recognizing when it's appropriate to step back entirely. There are times when being an ally involves working quietly behind the scenes, supporting efforts led by marginalized communities without needing visibility or recognition.

This process also requires an ally to recognize the difference between supporting marginalized voices and appropriating them. White men, and allies more broadly, must be mindful of the tendency to take up too much space or to speak on behalf of others. True allyship respects the autonomy and expertise of marginalized voices, avoiding the pitfall of becoming a "spokesperson" for experiences they do not live. This humility and respect for boundaries is essential to creating an environment where marginalized voices can genuinely flourish without interference or misrepresentation.

Listening is an essential skill in allyship, but it is also a deeply transformative practice for the listener. For white men, who have often been socialized into roles of authority and dominance, listening offers a pathway to connection and accountability. Through listening, they gain insight into the lives and struggles of those from marginalized backgrounds, recognizing their humanity in new and profound ways. It allows them to step outside of their own experiences, to develop empathy and understanding, and ultimately, to build meaningful relationships rooted in mutual respect and trust.

This chapter has highlighted the nuances of listening as an act of engagement, a deliberate choice to hear and support others as they express their truths. It is the foundation upon which all other aspects of allyship are built, providing a grounding in humility, emotional intelligence, and respect for the lived experiences of others. By listening well, allies lay the groundwork for a more equitable world, one where every voice has the space to be heard and valued.

Chapter 4: The Intersection of Race and Gender: Breaking Down Barriers

In social justice discussions, race and gender are often approached as separate issues, each with its own unique set of struggles and historical contexts. However, the reality of our lives is that identities do not exist in isolation; they overlap and intersect in complex ways. This is especially true for women of color, who experience the compounded effects of racial and gender discrimination. This chapter aims to explore the ways in which these intersections shape experiences, identities, and challenges and offers insights into how white men can better understand and ally themselves with women of color who navigate these compounded barriers daily.

As we dive into this intersection of race and gender, we'll address several key areas: the importance of intersectional theory as a framework for understanding layered identities, the ways in which privilege is a multi-dimensional experience, and practical steps that white men can take to support and amplify the voices of women of color as allies. Through this exploration, the chapter emphasizes that being an ally requires not just acknowledging the struggles of women of color but actively learning how to dismantle the unique forms of discrimination they face.

Intersectional theory provides a framework for understanding how different aspects of a person's identity—such as race, gender, class, sexuality, and more—intersect and create unique experiences of oppression and privilege. Coined by legal scholar Kimberlé Crenshaw in the late 1980s, intersectionality arose from the realization that existing legal frameworks failed to address the discrimination faced by Black women, which differed significantly from the experiences of white women or Black men. Crenshaw pointed out that both racial and gender discrimination were often treated as separate issues, which ignored the compounded challenges faced by those who belong to multiple marginalized groups.

For example, while a white woman might experience sexism in the workplace, her experiences differ from those of a Black woman, who may face both sexism and racial discrimination simultaneously. Intersectional theory teaches us that these overlapping identities do not simply add up to a "double burden" but instead create distinct experiences that need to be understood on their own terms. This is particularly important for white men seeking to understand how they can better support women of color, as it highlights the limitations of viewing race or gender in isolation.

In practice, adopting an intersectional perspective means recognizing that a "one-size-fits-all" approach to allyship is insufficient. White men who seek to support women of color must learn to see the world through an intersectional lens, understanding that the experiences of women of color differ from those of white women or men of color in ways that are both subtle and profound. Acknowledging intersectionality allows for a more inclusive and accurate understanding of how discrimination functions in society, making it possible to engage with social justice in ways that respect and uplift all identities involved.

The concept of privilege is central to discussions of race, gender, and social justice. Privilege, in this context, refers to the unearned advantages that individuals may have by virtue of their race, gender, or other aspects of their identity. White men, for instance, often enjoy privileges associated with both their race and gender, which afford them societal benefits that may be invisible to them but are starkly apparent to those who do not share these advantages.

When we talk about layered experiences of privilege, we are recognizing that privilege is not a simple, one-dimensional concept. A white man may experience the world differently than a white woman, due to his male privilege, and differently still from a Black man or a woman of color, who face both racial and gendered forms of discrimination. For white men seeking to become allies, understanding privilege as layered and intersectional is crucial, as it enables them to see how their own identities impact their perceptions of injustice and shapes their role within social justice movements.

One key aspect of layered privilege is the invisibility of certain privileges to those who hold them. Because privilege often functions as a default social position—one that does not need to be defended or explained—individuals with privilege may be unaware of how it affects their lives and interactions. White men, for example, may find it challenging to recognize the unique barriers faced by women of color in the workplace or in social spaces because they have never experienced these barriers firsthand. As allies, white men must actively work to become aware of the privileges they carry and recognize how these privileges shape their perspectives on social issues.

An important step in exploring layered privilege is understanding that allyship involves listening and learning. White men can benefit from examining their own assumptions and biases and acknowledging that they may not fully understand the realities faced by women of color. By approaching allyship with humility and a willingness to learn, white men can begin to build more authentic and supportive relationships with women of color, acknowledging both their own privilege and the unique challenges faced by those they seek to support.

True allyship is more than passive support or statements of solidarity. It involves active, ongoing efforts to understand the challenges faced by marginalized communities, amplify their voices, and advocate for change. For white men, becoming an ally to women—particularly women of color—requires a commitment to challenging their own assumptions, stepping back when necessary, and using their privilege to support others.

The first step to effective allyship is listening, a skill that is often overlooked but fundamental to understanding the experiences of others. White men who want to be allies to women of color must prioritize active listening, allowing women of color to share their experiences without judgment or defensiveness. This means resisting the urge to offer immediate solutions or question the validity of someone's experiences. Instead, effective allies focus on understanding, validating, and acknowledging what they hear.

In spaces where discussions of race and gender take place, white men often hold a disproportionate amount of influence. Effective allyship involves recognizing this influence and actively working to create space for women of color to share their perspectives and lead conversations. White men can do this by stepping back and allowing women of color to take leadership roles, advocating for their inclusion in decision-making spaces, and ensuring that they are not speaking over or diminishing the voices of those they seek to support.

One of the most important roles an ally can play is to educate themselves on issues of race, gender, and intersectionality. Rather than relying on women of color to explain their experiences or educate others, white men can take the initiative to read, attend workshops, and seek out resources that help them better understand intersectional oppression. Educating oneself is a lifelong process, and it demonstrates respect for the knowledge and experiences of marginalized communities.

White men who are committed to allyship should also be vigilant about identifying and challenging their own biases. Microaggressions—subtle, often unintentional actions or comments that reinforce stereotypes—are a common form of racial and gender-based discrimination. While these behaviors may seem minor, they accumulate over time and can have a profound impact on women of color. Allies must not only avoid perpetuating these microaggressions but also actively challenge them when they see them occur, even in social or professional settings.

Finally, allyship should extend beyond individual relationships and into advocacy for broader systemic change. White men in positions of influence, whether in workplaces, educational institutions, or government, can use their platforms to advocate for policies that support gender and racial equality. This may include supporting policies that promote diversity and inclusion, holding organizations accountable for discriminatory practices, or advocating for structural reforms that address systemic inequities faced by women of color.

The intersection of race and gender creates unique challenges for women of color, who navigate a world steeped in stereotypes and layered discrimination. For white men, understanding this intersectionality is essential to becoming a true ally. By embracing intersectional theory, examining their own layered privilege, and committing to active allyship, white men can help to dismantle the barriers that have long marginalized women of color. This journey requires empathy, humility, and a commitment to continuous growth. Allyship is not a destination but an evolving process—one that requires sustained effort, self-reflection, and a dedication to creating a world where all identities are respected, valued, and empowered.

Chapter 5: Redefining Masculinity and Privilege

In today's world, masculinity is being reconsidered and redefined. The traditional concept of masculinity, once associated with traits like dominance, control, stoicism, and aggression, is increasingly viewed as narrow and even harmful. These traits, particularly when emphasized to an extreme, can result in what is often called "toxic masculinity," a version of manhood that pressures men to assert dominance, shun vulnerability, and suppress emotional expression. For white men, especially, this traditional idea of masculinity has often intersected with racial privilege, reinforcing social structures that favor power over empathy and authority over equality.

This chapter explores the evolution of masculinity, focusing on how white men are beginning to question and reshape their identities in ways that support positive social change. By embracing "constructive" masculinity—characterized by empathy, vulnerability, cooperation, and self-reflection—men can engage in social movements in ways that promote inclusivity and equality. We will explore what it means to redefine masculinity, how white men can use this redefinition to confront privilege and engage meaningfully in social justice efforts, and why embracing vulnerability is key to building a more just and compassionate society.

"Toxic masculinity" refers to the harmful aspects of male identity rooted in cultural stereotypes that glorify dominance, aggression, and the suppression of emotions. It pressures men to see themselves as superior, as providers of strength who must avoid traits associated with femininity, like emotional openness or sensitivity. For many men, especially white men who have historically occupied positions of authority, this model of masculinity can reinforce a sense of entitlement to power and control, both personally and socially. Toxic masculinity promotes behaviors that can lead to aggression, suppression of emotions, and an aversion to vulnerability, ultimately isolating men from themselves and from others.

In contrast, constructive masculinity is a modern reimagining of what it means to be a man. Rather than defining strength as an absence of vulnerability or compassion, constructive masculinity views strength as the ability to embrace one's emotions, express empathy, and engage in relationships authentically. This model encourages men to see themselves as equal partners in relationships, both personal and societal, and to contribute to communities with an open and respectful mindset. It's a masculinity that values cooperation over control, empathy over assertion, and emotional health over stoicism.

For white men specifically, this shift toward constructive masculinity has broader implications. As they begin to redefine what it means to be masculine, they also start to challenge historical roles of power and privilege. Constructive masculinity does not see vulnerability or allyship as weaknesses but as essential strengths in creating meaningful change. By adopting these values, white men can become more effective allies in social justice movements, using their influence to amplify voices rather than dominate spaces.

Positive masculinity takes constructive masculinity a step further by actively focusing on how men can be a force for positive change. This version of masculinity encourages men to use their skills, knowledge, and privilege in ways that uplift others, foster inclusivity, and advocate for justice. It also emphasizes that being a man does not require distancing oneself from emotions or adhering to rigid social roles; rather, positive masculinity encourages men to redefine their identities in ways that align with values like equity, compassion, and respect for all genders.

White men in particular, when they embody positive masculinity, can play a powerful role in dismantling systemic inequality. Historically, many of the systems of power that enforce inequality were created and upheld by men. This history places a special responsibility on men—especially those with racial privilege—to challenge these systems by actively working to create environments of inclusion and accountability. Positive masculinity empowers men to be allies who understand that supporting change is about collaboration, not control.

Positive masculinity also rejects the notion of zero-sum power, which implies that if one group gains rights or visibility, another loses out. In positive masculinity, equity is a shared goal, not a competition. White men who embrace positive masculinity recognize that they do not need to "give up" their manhood or power to support change; instead, they need to shift their perspectives on what it means to be strong, compassionate, and responsible. This includes speaking up against inequality when they witness it, educating themselves on issues outside their own experience, and finding ways to support marginalized voices without taking center stage.

One of the core tenets of redefining masculinity is the idea of vulnerability. In traditional models of masculinity, vulnerability is often viewed as a weakness—a trait that makes a man "less manly." However, in constructive and positive masculinity, vulnerability is seen as a strength. Embracing vulnerability allows men to connect more deeply with themselves and others, opening the door to genuine empathy and understanding. For white men engaged in social justice, vulnerability means being willing to acknowledge privilege, confront biases, and listen to experiences different from their own without defensiveness.

Embracing vulnerability also allows men to step away from the pressures of perfectionism and authority that traditional masculinity imposes. By accepting that they don't need to have all the answers or always be in control, men can engage in learning and growth. Vulnerability, in this sense, is not a passive state but an active choice to be open and receptive to the realities that others face. It's a way of being that values personal growth and empathy over dominance and control.

This can be especially powerful in conversations about privilege, as it encourages white men to listen rather than react defensively when confronted with perspectives on inequality or discrimination. In practical terms, this might mean listening without interjecting, seeking to understand rather than to assert, and being willing to admit mistakes or gaps in understanding. Vulnerability also means accepting that allyship is a journey, one that requires continual reflection and a commitment to improvement.

By embracing vulnerability, white men can redefine strength as the courage to support others, to reflect on their own impact, and to accept the discomfort that comes with real growth. Vulnerability does not diminish masculinity; rather, it enhances it by fostering qualities like compassion, humility, and empathy—qualities that have the power to build stronger, more inclusive communities.

Redefining masculinity is not only beneficial on an individual level but has a wider impact on society and social movements. By challenging the traditional model of masculinity, white men can contribute to a culture that values inclusion, equity, and respect. This shift has significant implications for movements advocating for racial justice, gender equality, LGBTQ+ rights, and other forms of social change. When men bring constructive and positive masculinity to these spaces, they help to create environments where diverse voices are valued, and oppressive power dynamics are challenged.

For example, men in leadership positions who model empathy and vulnerability help to dismantle workplace cultures that prioritize aggression and control, making way for more collaborative and inclusive environments. White men who embrace positive masculinity can use their influence to advocate for policies that promote equity, challenge discrimination, and support marginalized groups. They can also educate other men on the importance of redefining masculinity, fostering a culture that sees allyship as a collective responsibility rather than an individual choice.

Moreover, by redefining masculinity, white men can become more attuned to their own identities and privileges. This self-awareness is crucial in a world where allyship requires not only solidarity but also accountability. When men are willing to hold themselves accountable, they set a powerful example for others, showing that strength lies not in domination but in integrity and respect. This redefinition of masculinity enables white men to engage in social movements not as figures of authority but as collaborators, committed to building a society rooted in justice and equality.

Redefining masculinity is a journey that requires courage, reflection, and a willingness to change. For white men, this journey also involves confronting the intersections of race, gender, and privilege, recognizing how these aspects of identity shape their roles within society. By moving away from toxic masculinity and embracing constructive and positive masculinity, white men can play a meaningful role in fostering inclusive social movements that prioritize empathy, respect, and equity.

This chapter has outlined a path forward for men who wish to redefine what it means to be masculine in ways that are inclusive, compassionate, and committed to positive change. Embracing vulnerability, supporting constructive masculinity, and embodying the values of allyship, white men can be active participants in creating a world where everyone—regardless of gender, race, or identity—is valued and respected. By reimagining masculinity, men have the opportunity not only to redefine themselves but also to reshape society for the better.

Chapter 6: Case Studies of Allyship and Resistance

Allyship is not simply a label but a series of actions, choices, and reflections that shape both individual and collective progress. Throughout history, white men have played various roles in social justice movements—some as staunch allies, others as resistant figures, and some whose well-intentioned actions inadvertently set back the very causes they intended to support. This chapter provides in-depth case studies of white men who have made significant impacts, analyzing both their successes and their failures. By looking at these figures closely, we aim to create a nuanced understanding of effective allyship, while also identifying common pitfalls that can inadvertently hinder progress.

John Brown was a white abolitionist whose radical and uncompromising stance on slavery in the United States placed him at odds with much of his society. Believing that slavery was a moral atrocity that could not be dismantled through peaceful means alone, Brown took part in armed resistance, most notably his raid on the federal armory at Harpers Ferry in 1859. Brown hoped his actions would incite a slave revolt, sparking a movement that could end slavery altogether.

Although his methods were controversial—many contemporaries condemned his use of violence—Brown's fierce commitment to equality left a lasting legacy. Brown demonstrated an unwavering allyship with Black Americans, to the extent of risking his own life and being executed for his actions. His dedication resonated with abolitionists, inspiring future generations of activists and marking him as a white ally who genuinely understood the gravity of systemic oppression. While historians debate the ethics of his violent tactics, Brown's actions exemplify the power of uncompromising commitment to a cause, as well as the potential of allyship to challenge deeply entrenched injustices.

In the summer of 1964, Andrew Goodman and Michael Schwerner, two white men from New York, joined James Chaney, a Black activist from Mississippi, as part of the Freedom Summer campaign. Their goal was to register Black voters in the racially hostile South. Tragically, all three were murdered by members of the Ku Klux Klan in Philadelphia, Mississippi, after being arrested and released by local law enforcement who were complicit in the act. The deaths of Goodman, Schwerner, and Chaney became a rallying cry for the Civil Rights Movement and galvanized support across the nation.

Their sacrifice highlighted the risks that white allies could face when standing up against systemic racism, especially in areas where racial tensions were at their peak. By putting their lives on the line and refusing to turn away from injustice, Goodman and Schwerner became symbols of white allyship that was willing to face extreme personal danger. Their actions, in tandem with Chaney's, underscored the powerful effect of cross-racial solidarity and illustrated that allyship sometimes requires putting oneself in harm's way to challenge oppression directly.

Tim Wise is a contemporary anti-racist educator whose work has focused on exploring the history and psychology of white privilege and its impacts on racial inequality. Wise has spent his career unpacking the subtle and overt ways in which white privilege permeates institutions and individuals' lives. He uses his background and experience to confront other white people with the realities of privilege, working to raise awareness and provoke introspection.

Wise's approach has been largely successful, reaching mainstream audiences through books, lectures, and media. He demonstrates how white men can use their positions of privilege to speak to other white people in ways that may be less accessible to non-white voices. By leveraging his identity as a white man, Wise has been able to reach audiences who may otherwise resist conversations about racism. However, his role is not without criticism; some argue that he occasionally centers himself and his own voice within the anti-racist movement. Nonetheless, Wise's work provides an example of allyship that uses education as a tool to confront bias and prejudice within the white community, offering insights into how white allies can contribute effectively to the fight for racial justice.

The American rapper Macklemore offers a case study in well-intentioned allyship that, despite good intentions, may have hindered more than helped. Known for his hit song "Same Love," which addressed LGBTQ+ rights and became an anthem for the marriage equality movement, Macklemore was celebrated as an ally for his willingness to speak out on social issues. However, some critics noted that his success in addressing LGBTQ+ issues drew attention and resources toward a straight, white man, rather than uplifting voices within the LGBTQ+ community itself.

Macklemore's experience highlights a common challenge in allyship: the potential for allies to inadvertently center themselves within a movement rather than the individuals and communities the movement is meant to empower. While his music helped raise awareness, the outsized attention he received illustrated how easy it is for well-meaning allies to overshadow marginalized voices. His case serves as a cautionary tale about the importance of amplifying voices within the communities affected by injustice, rather than positioning oneself as the "face" of a movement.

These case studies not only illustrate what effective allyship can look like but also highlight key pitfalls that can hinder progress. Macklemore's case, for instance, shows how centering oneself, even with good intentions, can detract from the movement's message. Similarly, the sometimes controversial approach of Tim Wise reminds us that even allies with valuable perspectives must continually check their roles and impacts. Other common mistakes include:

- **Speaking over marginalized voices:** Allies must learn to listen and understand when it is their place to speak and when it is better to pass the microphone to those directly affected.
- **Focusing on personal guilt or redemption:** Allies who become overly focused on absolving their own guilt may inadvertently make social justice about their own feelings, detracting from the work that needs to be done.
- **Overreliance on "good intentions":** While intentions matter, they do not erase impact. Even allies who mean well can contribute to harm if they are not attuned to the nuanced needs of the communities they seek to support.

Learning from these mistakes allows allies to approach movements with humility, openness, and a genuine commitment to making a positive impact.

Effective allyship can create far-reaching ripple effects within social movements. For instance, when white allies like Goodman and Schwerner joined the Freedom Summer movement, their participation brought national attention to the voting rights struggle in the South, inspiring widespread support. Similarly, Tim Wise's work in anti-racist education has helped catalyze conversations on privilege among white audiences who might have been reluctant to engage with these topics.

However, even seemingly small missteps can have ripple effects, too. Macklemore's experience, while well-intentioned, demonstrated how centering a white voice within the LGBTQ+ movement could inadvertently reinforce the same dynamics of privilege that the movement sought to dismantle.

Allyship's potential lies in its ability to model accountability, empathy, and support within a broader movement. When executed thoughtfully and with an understanding of the complex dynamics at play, it can help accelerate social progress. Allies who understand the ripple effects of their actions—both positive and negative—are better equipped to make thoughtful, impactful contributions to social justice.

The stories of John Brown, Goodman and Schwerner, Tim Wise, and Macklemore illustrate the complexities of allyship and provide a roadmap for how white men can engage with social justice movements responsibly and effectively. By examining these figures, this chapter underscores the importance of self-awareness, the need to avoid centering oneself, and the power of allyship that is grounded in a commitment to amplifying marginalized voices. True allyship requires humility, the willingness to confront uncomfortable truths, and a dedication to placing the needs of the movement above personal accolades. Through thoughtful engagement and continuous learning, white men can contribute to a more just and equitable society for all.

Chapter 7: Facing Backlash and Controversy

In the journey of allyship, one of the most challenging and inevitable experiences for white men is facing backlash and controversy. Engaging with social justice and identity movements often involves navigating uncomfortable truths, reconciling past and present privileges, and adjusting to new perspectives. This chapter explores how these challenges manifest as backlash, how white men can approach criticism constructively, and how to move beyond fragility to contribute meaningfully to the fight for equality and justice.

As social movements call for transformative changes, they frequently challenge established norms and power structures. This change is naturally met with resistance, sometimes even from those attempting to support the movement. In the case of white men, "allyship backlash" can emerge both from internal struggles with privilege and external critiques from marginalized communities. This backlash takes multiple forms and is crucial to understand for any white man striving to be a genuine ally.

At its core, allyship backlash refers to the reactions—both defensive and reflexive—that arise when an individual with privilege attempts to participate in social movements but encounters resistance, scrutiny, or perceived rejection. It can stem from feelings of guilt, inadequacy, or defensiveness, particularly when allies face criticism from the communities they aim to support. These reactions are often rooted in discomfort around unlearning ingrained biases and reckoning with personal and collective histories. Allyship backlash is a byproduct of moving through this discomfort, an indication that a deeper reckoning is taking place.

For example, many white men experience "performative ally" accusations—criticisms that suggest their actions are superficial or primarily for social approval. This kind of backlash can be difficult to process, especially for individuals who genuinely want to contribute. Rather than disengaging, white men can use these moments as opportunities for self-reflection and growth, recognizing that criticisms often stem from a place of lived experience and frustration with historical patterns of empty gestures. Understanding the sources and contexts of these criticisms allows white men to learn from them, avoiding superficial actions and deepening their allyship.

Another common form of allyship backlash is when white men encounter resentment or distrust within activist communities, especially if they inadvertently act in ways that center their own voices. Historically, many social justice movements have been led by marginalized groups who carry the lived experiences that shape these causes. When allies fail to recognize this history or assert themselves too prominently, it can reinforce the very power dynamics the movement seeks to dismantle. Rather than seeing this as rejection, allies must learn to approach these situations as reminders to step back and listen, making space for voices that are essential to the movement's integrity.

Criticism is an integral part of growth, but learning to accept and grow from it is a skill that requires humility and resilience. For white men engaging in social movements, criticism often feels personal. It can lead to defensiveness or a desire to withdraw from the work. However, if viewed constructively, criticism can be one of the most valuable resources for meaningful allyship.

The first step in dealing with criticism is to shift perspective: rather than seeing it as an attack, view it as a gift. Criticism from marginalized communities, while it may be difficult to hear, is usually rooted in a lifetime of experience, observation, and accumulated frustration with systems of oppression. In listening to these critiques, white men have a unique opportunity to learn directly from those most affected by the issues they are seeking to support.

An essential element of handling criticism is recognizing when and why defensiveness arises. Often, the desire to defend oneself is tied to fragility—the discomfort that comes from confronting one's own role in oppressive systems. While fragility is a natural response, allies must work to set it aside, as defensiveness can act as a barrier to growth. By acknowledging fragility and consciously choosing to listen instead of react, white men can engage with feedback in a constructive way. A practical approach might involve developing a "pause and reflect" mindset: when criticism arises, pause before responding. Take time to assess whether the reaction is rooted in defensiveness and how it might be transformed into a learning moment.

Another useful strategy is to approach criticism with curiosity. Ask questions that promote understanding, and avoid "Yes, but..." responses, which can often come across as dismissive. For instance, rather than responding to criticism with, "I didn't mean it that way," allies might ask, "Can you help me understand how that came across?" Such questions can open a dialogue, showing a willingness to learn without placing the burden of education entirely on marginalized communities.

Criticism can also serve as a lens for examining one's intentions. When criticized, it's natural to feel misunderstood, but taking the time to examine why one feels the need to "prove" good intentions can be illuminating. Being an ally isn't about seeking validation; it's about contributing to meaningful change. Allies must ask themselves, "Am I seeking to understand, or am I seeking reassurance?" This shift in mindset can create a more resilient foundation for continued involvement in social justice work.

Fragility is often one of the most significant hurdles white men face in social justice work. It manifests as discomfort, defensiveness, and, in some cases, complete withdrawal when faced with difficult truths about privilege and systemic oppression. Fragility is not a flaw unique to any one group; it's a human reaction to confronting uncomfortable realities. However, recognizing and addressing fragility is essential for white men who wish to be effective allies.

At its root, fragility stems from a dissonance between self-perception and the reality of privilege. For example, a white man may perceive himself as someone who values equality and fairness. When confronted with the idea that he might inadvertently perpetuate systems of oppression, this dissonance creates an emotional response, often expressed as fragility. Understanding that fragility is a natural response rather than a personal failing can help allies work through it rather than retreat from it.

Moving past fragility involves developing resilience—the ability to face criticism, discomfort, and confrontation without retreating into defensiveness. One way to build resilience is by regularly practicing self-reflection and cultivating an awareness of one's own biases. This means not only reflecting on personal beliefs but also examining how those beliefs translate into behaviors. Regularly asking questions like, "How might my actions be perceived by others?" or "Am I unconsciously centering myself in this discussion?" can help allies avoid pitfalls of fragility.

Moreover, resilience in allyship often requires cultivating empathy and emotional regulation. When white men encounter moments of discomfort, the instinct might be to justify, defend, or rationalize their actions. Developing the capacity to sit with discomfort, feel it fully, and then respond thoughtfully rather than reactively is a mark of a strong ally. Practices like mindfulness can be particularly helpful in managing emotions and reducing the impulse to respond defensively.

Another important aspect of overcoming fragility is understanding the impact of collective history. White men must recognize that discomfort or hurt feelings often pale in comparison to the lived experiences of those who face systemic injustice every day. Putting fragility into perspective helps allies realize that personal discomfort is a small price to pay in the pursuit of a fairer society. This perspective fosters a sense of humility and strengthens the commitment to the cause, reinforcing the idea that allyship is about something much larger than individual feelings.

In this chapter, we've explored how backlash and criticism can serve as catalysts for growth, rather than barriers. Allyship requires a willingness to embrace discomfort, listen with humility, and learn from critiques without centering oneself in the movement. White men who are willing to engage with backlash, face their own fragility, and work through criticism constructively can find themselves contributing in more impactful ways, creating a foundation for allyship that is rooted in resilience, empathy, and commitment to true equity.

In moving past backlash and fragility, white men can become more than just allies—they can become accomplices in the fight for justice, actively supporting systemic change. The path isn't easy, and mistakes are inevitable, but with perseverance and an open mind, they can meaningfully participate in movements that reshape the world for the better.

Chapter 8: A Vision for the Future

As we closer to the end of this book, we arrive at a pivotal moment. The previous chapters have examined history, societal structures, identity, privilege, and the complex roles that white men play in social, racial, gender, and identity movements. We have explored both contributions and challenges, the process of allyship, and the need for empathy and listening. Now, we look ahead, envisioning a future where the commitment to equality and justice is woven into the fabric of society—a world where allyship is practiced at every level and where diverse voices are valued and empowered.

This chapter outlines a roadmap for future engagement, highlighting how white men can continue to grow within these movements and contribute meaningfully. Building this future requires sustained self-reflection, active participation in allyship, and a dedication to creating a society rooted in mutual respect and equality. The journey does not end with awareness or one-time actions; it calls for a lifelong commitment to understanding and embracing the complexities of an inclusive world.

True allyship and engagement start with knowledge. One of the most crucial aspects of evolving within social justice movements is a commitment to ongoing education, particularly around issues of race, gender, and identity. For white men, this means continuously exploring both the external and internal factors that shape privilege, bias, and societal dynamics. Self-education is an essential part of recognizing one's own position within a broader social system. Without it, there is a risk of unconsciously reinforcing stereotypes, assumptions, or actions that may hinder progress.

Self-education is not about checking off a list of readings or attending a single workshop; it's a lifelong practice of curiosity and critical reflection. White men who are serious about contributing to these movements should remain engaged with relevant literature, follow thought leaders from diverse backgrounds, and actively participate in conversations about social justice. Educational materials are constantly evolving, as new voices, perspectives, and research emerge. A commitment to self-education is a commitment to understanding these new insights and integrating them into one's worldview.

Furthermore, self-education involves learning to critically examine societal norms and personal biases. This process may reveal uncomfortable truths, but it is essential for growth. Each individual has unique experiences and beliefs, some of which may be shaped by a privileged position in society. Confronting these truths with honesty allows white men to better understand the role they play in perpetuating or challenging inequality, and it empowers them to act with greater awareness and empathy.

Allyship is more than just supporting social movements from the sidelines; it requires active participation and a willingness to stand alongside marginalized communities, often in ways that are challenging and complex. In envisioning a future of equality and justice, white men must find both personal and collective meaning in allyship. They must see it not as a performative act or a badge of honor, but as a deeply held commitment to justice.

On a personal level, allyship means recognizing that everyone has a stake in creating a just society. For white men, this often involves understanding that while they may not face the same challenges as marginalized communities, they are still deeply connected to the structures of privilege that shape society. By confronting these realities, they can find a sense of purpose in using their voices, resources, and influence to support meaningful change. Embracing this purpose is key to avoiding the performative traps of allyship, where actions are driven by a desire for approval rather than a commitment to equity.

At a collective level, allyship is about working within one's own communities to foster greater understanding and empathy. This might mean engaging with friends, family, colleagues, or even broader social networks to discuss issues of inequality and challenge harmful narratives. When white men take on the role of educators within their circles, they can help shift cultural attitudes and expand the reach of social justice movements. By working collectively, they can amplify marginalized voices and contribute to building a society that values equality, compassion, and respect.

Additionally, collective allyship requires humility. It's vital for allies to acknowledge that they are not the center of the movements they support. By focusing on the perspectives and experiences of those directly impacted by social injustices, white men can act in ways that uplift others rather than overshadow them. This selfless approach to allyship helps build trust and reinforces the authenticity of one's commitment to justice.

Ultimately, the goal of engagement in social, racial, gender, and identity movements is to create a society where all individuals can thrive and live with dignity, equality, and respect. This vision extends beyond individual actions, calling for systemic change in education, politics, media, and social structures. White men, particularly those in positions of influence, have a responsibility to actively support policies and initiatives that contribute to a more inclusive world.

A more inclusive society requires that equity is embedded in the institutions that shape our lives. This can involve supporting educational reforms that teach a more accurate and inclusive history, advocating for equitable hiring practices that foster diversity, or championing policies that dismantle systemic biases in law enforcement and the justice system. These systemic changes are essential for addressing the root causes of inequality and creating lasting impact.

White men can also contribute to inclusivity by championing diverse leadership in various sectors. By supporting leaders from marginalized backgrounds and creating spaces where diverse perspectives are valued, they can help shift the dynamics of power that have historically excluded underrepresented voices. This is not about tokenism but about recognizing the value of diverse leadership and the benefits it brings to organizations and society as a whole.

Beyond institutional change, a more inclusive society requires a shift in cultural attitudes. White men can contribute to this by challenging stereotypes, calling out discriminatory behavior, and promoting empathy and understanding within their communities. Small actions, like speaking up when witnessing prejudice or encouraging open conversations about identity and privilege, can contribute to a cultural shift that fosters greater inclusivity.

Finally, building an inclusive society is also about creating spaces for future generations to continue this work. White men can support initiatives that empower youth, provide mentorship for young leaders from diverse backgrounds, and encourage younger generations to engage with issues of social justice. By investing in the next generation, they help ensure that the work of allyship and equality will continue to evolve and adapt to new challenges.

The path toward a just and inclusive society is an ongoing journey, one that requires dedication, humility, and a willingness to confront uncomfortable truths. For white men, this journey involves recognizing privilege, committing to self-education, finding personal and collective meaning in allyship, and actively working to build a world where everyone has the opportunity to thrive. This vision is not an endpoint but a continuous process of growth and engagement. Each step taken, whether small or large, contributes to the broader movement for social justice.

As we prepare to move to the last chapter of this book, it offers an invitation: to each reader, and especially to white men, to envision the future not as a distant ideal but as a reality they have the power to shape today. Through intentional action, empathy, and a commitment to equality, white men can play a crucial role in moving society toward a more just and inclusive world for generations to come.

Chapter 9: The Journey Toward Social Justice

The road to social justice and equality is far from linear. It is a winding path, filled with obstacles, setbacks, and challenges, but also moments of growth, solidarity, and transformation. The journey toward a more just and equitable world requires more than just intention—it demands action, reflection, and an openness to change, even when that change requires us to confront uncomfortable truths about ourselves and the world around us. Throughout this book, we have explored the multifaceted roles that white men play in social, racial, gender, and identity movements, offering a nuanced view of both the opportunities and challenges they face along the way.

The idea that this journey is not a straight line is crucial to understanding the complexity of allyship and social justice work. It would be easy to assume that there is a clear, right path to follow, one that guarantees immediate success and flawless execution. However, as we have seen, the reality is much more complicated. There will be mistakes. There will be moments when you stumble, when you fail to understand the full implications of your actions, or when your privilege blinds you to the needs and voices of others. But perhaps the greatest mistake is not the occasional misstep; the greatest mistake is not taking the journey at all.

We are all human, and we all come with our biases, our histories, and our limitations. None of us, especially white men, are immune to the structural systems of oppression that have shaped our world for centuries. However, it is in the willingness to engage with these systems, to confront our own role in perpetuating inequality, and to seek to make meaningful change that we find the potential for growth—not only for ourselves but for society as a whole.

Mistakes will be made—this is a certainty. We may speak out of turn, we may fail to fully listen, we may inadvertently perpetuate harmful stereotypes, or we may, at times, feel defensive when our privileges are called into question. These mistakes are not signs of failure, but rather opportunities for learning. They offer us the chance to examine our own biases and to grow beyond them. The key, however, is not to let these mistakes discourage us or cause us to abandon the journey entirely. Each misstep is a moment to reflect, to adjust, and to move forward with greater wisdom and compassion.

It is essential to remember that the goal of this journey is not perfection but progress. Social justice work is inherently uncomfortable at times, especially for those who benefit from systems of privilege. But as we face that discomfort head-on, we gain the perspective necessary to effect real, lasting change. Progress is measured not in grand gestures or a flawless track record but in the commitment to keep moving, to keep learning, and to keep standing in solidarity with those whose voices have been silenced for too long.

In the context of white men's roles in social movements, the potential for positive impact is immense, but it requires an unwavering commitment to personal accountability and a willingness to step aside when necessary. It means creating space for the voices of marginalized communities and using the privilege we hold to amplify rather than overshadow those voices. The journey asks us to redefine what it means to be an ally—not as a position of power, but as one of humility, respect, and support. It asks us to recognize that our own identities as white men are not static but fluid, shaped by our actions and choices.

Perhaps the most important lesson to take away from this journey is that the fight for justice is collective. It is not an individual endeavor but a communal one, where each person's contributions—no matter how small—add up to create a more inclusive, compassionate world. While the path may be difficult and full of uncertainty, it is a journey that is worth taking. And no matter how far you may stray or how many times you falter, it is always possible to return to that path, to continue learning, and to deepen your commitment to a just society.

By examining the history and potential of white men's roles in social movements, this book has sought to offer a roadmap for understanding and empathy. The hope is that this guide serves as a starting point for readers, urging them to engage with the work of justice—not just as a theoretical concept but as a lived experience. The goal is not only to build a society that is equitable for all people but to create a future in which everyone, regardless of race, gender, or identity, has the opportunity to thrive.

As we look toward the future, the journey toward social justice and equality is ongoing. Each generation has its own responsibility to carry the torch forward, to challenge the status quo, and to fight for a world where freedom, dignity, and opportunity are available to all. For white men, this journey requires both humility and strength—humility to listen, to learn, and to understand the experiences of those who have been oppressed, and strength to act, to stand firm in the face of resistance, and to continue moving forward when the road gets tough.

The work does not end with this book. It continues in the conversations you have, the actions you take, and the choices you make every day. Social justice and equality are not ideals that can be achieved overnight, but they are ideals worth fighting for. And while the journey is long and fraught with challenges, it is a journey that ultimately leads to a better world for everyone. The biggest mistake is not taking that first step. The most important thing is to continue moving forward, learning from the past, and working toward a future where justice, equality, and dignity are truly realized for all.

Educational Resources:
Books

1. **White Fragility: Why It's So Hard for White People to Talk About Racism** by Robin DiAngelo
    - Explores the defensiveness often experienced by white people in discussions about race and offers tools for building more productive dialogues.
2. **How to Be an Antiracist** by Ibram X. Kendi
    - Encourages readers to go beyond passive allyship and understand the difference between "not racist" and actively anti-racist behaviors.
3. **Me and White Supremacy** by Layla F. Saad
    - Originally a workbook, this book offers daily exercises and reflections to help readers identify and challenge their internalized biases.
4. **The Will to Change: Men, Masculinity, and Love** by bell hooks
    - Analyzes toxic masculinity and how men can transform their understanding of gender justice and self-worth.
5. **Man Enough: Undefining My Masculinity** by Justin Baldoni
    - A deeply personal exploration of masculinity, vulnerability, and how men can challenge traditional gender roles.
6. **Between the World and Me** by Ta-Nehisi Coates
    - Written as a letter to Coates' son, this memoir offers an intimate view of the Black American experience and systemic oppression.

Articles and Essays

1. **"White Privilege: Unpacking the Invisible Knapsack"** by

Peggy McIntosh
- A seminal essay on recognizing white privilege and understanding its impacts.
2. **"Men and #MeToo: Mapping White Masculinity in a Post-#MeToo World"** (Harvard Business Review)
    - Discusses white men's role in combating gender inequality and the #MeToo movement.
3. **"What Is White Privilege, Really?"** (Teaching Tolerance by Learning for Justice)
    - Breaks down the concept of white privilege and its societal implications with accessible examples.
4. **"10 Things Allies Can Do"** by Showing Up for Racial Justice (SURJ)
    - Provides practical steps white allies can take to support racial justice.

Courses and Workshops

1. **The Allyship & Action Summit**
    - An annual virtual summit focused on allyship, activism, and social justice, offering various resources, panels, and speakers on issues of privilege and allyship.
2. **The Antiracism Project** by Surge Institute
    - A six-session online course that dives into systemic racism and personal accountability for social change.
3. **"Seeing White" Podcast Series**
    - Examines the history and construction of "whiteness" and how it shapes society.
4. **Exploring Masculinities Course** by The Representation Project
    - An educational course that tackles themes of masculinity and social justice, helping men to reflect on their roles in gender equality.

Documentaries and Films

1. **13th**
    - Directed by Ava DuVernay, this documentary explores the intersection of race, justice, and mass incarceration in the United States.
2. **The Mask You Live In**
    - Focuses on the societal pressures men face in defining masculinity and the impact of these norms on mental health and identity.
3. **I Am Not Your Negro**
    - Based on the writings of James Baldwin, this film examines the history of racial discrimination in the U.S. through Baldwin's perspective.
4. **The Color of Fear**
    - A documentary about a group of men discussing racism and privilege, providing raw, honest insights into the dynamics of race and identity.

Websites and Online Resources

1. **Showing Up for Racial Justice (SURJ)**
    - An organization providing resources, action steps, and educational materials specifically for white people committed to fighting racial injustice.
2. **The Good Men Project**
    - Focused on defining modern masculinity, with articles and resources that discuss allyship, gender justice, and racial equality.
3. **Racial Equity Tools**
    - Offers resources, guides, and tools for understanding racial equity, structured to assist individuals and organizations in making effective social change.

4. **Project Implicit** (Harvard University)
    - Hosts the Implicit Association Test (IAT), which can help users explore their unconscious biases related to race, gender, and other identities.
5. **Teaching Tolerance (Learning for Justice)**
    - Provides articles, guides, and educational tools designed to help people better understand and confront issues of social injustice.

These resources cover history, allyship, masculinity, and privilege and offer both theoretical frameworks and practical actions. They can serve to expand an individual's understanding to their role in supporting social, racial, and gender justice movements.